Beginner Biography

by Bridges

A Brave Child Who Made History

by Jeri Cipriano
illustrated by Scott R. Brooks

Red Chair Press Egremont, M

Look! Books are produced and published by Red Chair Press:

Red Chair Press LLC   PO Box 333   South Egremont, MA 01258-0333

www.redchairpress.com

 FREE lesson guide at www.redchairpress.com/free-activities

Publisher's Cataloging-In-Publication Data

Names: Cipriano, Jeri S., author. | Brooks, Scott R., 1963- illustrator.

Title: Ruby Bridges: a brave child who made history / by Jeri Cipriano; illustrated by Scott R. Brooks.

Description: Egremont, Massachusetts : Red Chair Press, [2020] | Series: Look! books. Beginner biography | Includes index and resources for further reading. | Interest age level: 005-008. | Summary: "Ruby Bridges just wanted to go to a good school. She did not ask to be a hero, but she knew how to be strong. Her bravery made it possible for classrooms today to be safe places for children of all races."--Provided by publisher.

Identifiers: ISBN 9781634409636 (library hardcover) | ISBN 9781634409643 (paperback) | ISBN 9781634409650 (ebook)

Subjects: LCSH: Bridges, Ruby--Juvenile literature. | African American children--Louisiana--New Orleans--Biography--Juvenile literature. | African Americans--Education--Louisiana--New Orleans--Juvenile literature. | School integration--United States--History--20th century--Juvenile literature. | CYAC: Bridges, Ruby. | African American children--Louisiana--New Orleans--Biography. | African Americans--Education--Louisiana--New Orleans. | School integration--United States--History--20th century.

Classification: LCC F379.N59 N436 2020 (print) | LCC F379.N59 (ebook) | DDC 379.2/63/092 B--dc23

Library of Congress Control Number: 2019938786

Photo credits: GettyImages: 4; Alamy: 20

Printed in the United States of America

0819 1P CGS20

Table of Contents

Introduction

Years ago, black children and white children did not go to school together. They did not live in the same neighborhoods. They never had a chance to meet and become friends.

In some states, there were **laws** that kept black people and white people apart.

WE WONT GO TO SCHOOL WITH NEGROES

This child's sign shows that white people did not welcome children (**Negroes**) in their schools.

Even when new laws replaced the old ones, many people stuck to old ways.

Ruby was just a little girl, but she wasn't afraid to face big bullies on her way to school each day.

Ruby: The Early Years

Ruby Nell Bridges was born on September 8, 1954, in Tylertown, Mississippi. Ruby lived with her parents and grandparents on a farm.

Ruby's parents did not go to school. They decided to move to a big city so Ruby could go to school.

Ruby's family moved to New Orleans. Ruby's dad got a job at a gas station. Her mother worked nights.

Ruby's mother kisses Ruby and her brothers and sister good night before leaving for work.

New Orleans

Ruby went to kindergarten in New Orleans. All her classmates were black.

She liked school. She had friends to play with during **recess** each day.

A New Law Brings Change

In 1954, the **Supreme Court** ruled that states could not have separate schools for black and white children. The Court said that *separate* schools were not *equal*.

Good to Know

Ruby took a test. The test showed which black children could go to white schools.

Little Ruby Takes a Big Step

Ruby's father didn't want her to go to the white kids' school. He was afraid of trouble. But her mother thought Ruby would be a good example for other black children to follow.

Ruby was one of the first black children to enter an all-white school. The whole town showed up to keep her out. But Ruby made up her mind to do the right thing. She was only six years old.

Ruby walked right up the steps into the school. Some men were there to protect her form the crowd.

First Grade

November 14, 1960, was Ruby's first day at the all-white elementary school.

Angry crowds of white people were gathered on Ruby's way to school. They shouted at her. Big, tall white men protected Ruby by standing close.

Good to Know

One police officer said Ruby never cried. "She just marched along like a little soldier," he said.

Alone in Class

Ruby was the only black child at the school. But there were only a few white children, too.

Most parents took their children out of the school. Some worried about safety. But most took their children out of the school to **protest** having Ruby there.

17

Second Grade and Beyond

By second grade, things got easier for Ruby. She walked to school without needing grownups. She made friends.

Ruby continued to go to schools with both black and white students.

Today, Ruby is married with four sons. She visits schools around the country and tells her story.

In 2011, Ruby met President Barack Obama at the White House in a historic moment.

Timeline: Big Dates in Ruby's Life

1954: Ruby Bridges is born in Mississippi.

1954: It becomes against the law to put black children and white children in different schools.

1960: Ruby becomes the first black child to go to an all-white school in the South.

1961: Ruby goes to second grade. Black and white children go to school together peacefully.

1963: Norman Rockwell paints a picture that shows Ruby's courage.

1964: The Rockwell painting appears on the cover of Look Magazine. It is titled "The Problem We All Live With."

1984: Ruby marries Malcolm Hall. They raise four boys.

1995: Ruby and her first-grade teacher, Mrs. Henry, meet as grownups.

2011: Ruby meets the first black US President at the White House.

Words to Know

laws: rules that people in a community or country must follow

Negro: a word used before the 1970s to refer to dark-skinned people

protest: to complain strongly

recess: a break between school classes; a time for play

Supreme Court: the highest court in the United States

Learn More at the Library

(Check out these books to read with others.)

Bridges, Ruby. *Ruby Bridges Goes to School: My True Story.* Scholastic, 2016.

Donaldson, Madeline. *Ruby Bridges.* Lerner, 2009.

Ribke, Simone T. *Ruby Bridges (Rookie Biographies).* Children's Press, 2015.

Index

About the Author

Jeri Cipriano has written more than a hundred books for young readers. She enjoys reading and finding out new things. She likes to share what she learns.